FRAGMENTS
FROM THE BIG PIECE

A PLAY

. . . . IN

EIGHT SCENES

BY . . . .

BRIAN KAUFMAN

[signature: Brian Kaufman]
16-01-95

ANVIL PRESS
PERFORMANCE SERIES

FRAGMENTS FROM THE BIG PIECE
Copyright © 1989, 1991 Brian Kaufman

Published by Anvil Press
P.O. Box 1575, Station A
Vancouver, B.C., CANADA
V6C 2P7

Fragments from the Big Piece was first produced by Dark Horse Theatre, Vancouver, in 1989.

CANADIAN CATALOGUING IN PUBLICATION DATA

Kaufman, Brian, 1956–
Fragments from the big piece

    (Anvil performance series, ISSN 1188-0872 ; no. 1)
    ISBN 1-895636-02-7

    I. Title.   II. Series.
PS8571.A93F7 1991   C812'.54   C92-091002-5
PR9199.3.K36F7 1991

Cover Design: Gek-Bee Siou

Printed & bound in Canada.

For Karen

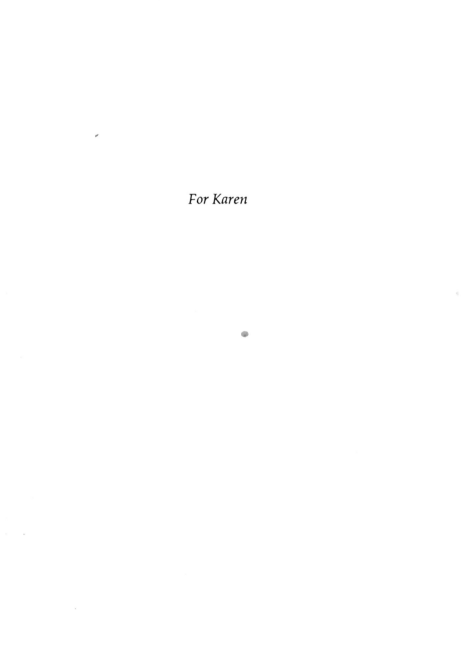

Fragments from the Big Piece was first produced by Dark Horse Theatre at the 1989 Vancouver Fringe Festival. The production was directed by David U. Garfinkle with the following cast:

BETTY	*Jennifer Griffin*
STORYTELLER	*Nona Avren*
BRAD	*Tom Edwards*
LYDIA	*Ethel Whitty*
THE INFORMATIONIST	*Stephanie Boyd*
THE SHIV	*David Wilson*
LEO	*David Wilson*
FAT MAN	*Ian Ross McDonald*
JIMMY	*Dean Haglund*
DR. MARTIN	*Stephanie Boyd*

Vice Captain	*Scott Davis*
Saxophone Player	*Marko Guizzo*

PRELUDE

Sound of rain. BETTY *moves slowly downstage, silhouetted by a single spot. She is wearing a tight, racy dress. She is soaking wet, cold. She is barefoot, carrying her shoes; one has a broken spike. Her reading is punctuated by short spurts of angry sax.*

BASTARDS!
All men

S T I L L . . . .

Hello, I love you
No! Don't tell me
Your name
I don't want
To know

Time ripping at me
Tearing me
Away
All for unpaid
Debts
Of youth

And what can it be
That I'm doing?
Standing
In the rain
Heart torn
And broken shoe
My dress, my body
Dripping
Glass
Churning in my guts

Brazen little tarts
With youth
in their tits
BUST THEM UP!

Show them something
Of life

Where does it lead?
How does it end?
What can it be
that I'm doing?
Maybe
Yes, just maybe
I'm building
The perfect
Mousetrap

And how does it end?
With me
A knife
My hand

Lights snap to black.

Utilizing either slides or a film clip: various shots taken of the characters attending a burial service: group dressed in black, shots from various angles; several close-ups, shots of bouquet being tossed to the casket, handful of earth; several of the characters getting into cars. This is accompanied by house music: something along the lines of Adagio for strings, Op.11, by Samuel Barber. OR: Scene executed on stage, accompanied by pianist or taped music. After last slide dissolves, the music stops. The video monitor, centre stage, snaps on, to a close-up of wood burning. Amplified sound of a faucet dripping into a pool of water.

Enter STORYTELLER. He stands in front of the monitor. He is rubbing his shoulders, blowing into cupped hands, trying to stay warm. Wind whistling gently. He approaches the monitor and warms his hands at the fire. Shortly after the STORYTELLER begins his opening speech, a computer printer starts churning out sheets of data.

STORYTELLER: I had a theory. A theory so *big*, so *fantastic*, it went without saying that I was going to be immensely wealthy and famous. Interviews, talk shows, the lecture circuit—it was all there. All easily within my grasp. The *Journal of Social Psychology* had even requested excerpts from my forthcoming text. My publisher, in a rare act of charity, managed to procure an advance of several *thousand*—with nothing more than a ten-page synopsis. 'To get my butt in the chair,' as he put it, to get those more or less *abstract notions* into some sort of concrete form. Fine, just what I needed—incentive. And it worked . . . for a while. But, premature praise and compensation are not the best kindling for the flames of inspiration. After all, it was only an *idea*. It hadn't been fully developed, brought to fruition. But they wanted it *out there*, molded into some sort of product, something the masses could consume. I pulled back. Naturally. Well, to be quite truthful, I was beginning to have doubts, serious doubts. I was nervous about what I was putting out there, how it might be used. Did I dare unleash such an incredible idea upon the impressionable minds of humanity? And it was all too rushed. They didn't understand that these things take *time*. The research was going badly—I was in a slump. I didn't have a single case study to support my claim—I had no practical basis in reality. So, like any intelligent, slightly unstable North American coward, I resorted to that favourite pastime of the celebratory few and the mourning masses: *drinking*. The Vacant Lot, a lounge on the Eastside, became my study, my sanctuary, my *laboratory*. I drank and thought and thought and drank, and drank some more, and—I *talked*. Always secretly in search of that *condition*, that particular *disorder* to bolster my theory. But . . . inevitably the months stumbled by. The Lot was no longer vacant, with all the rounds I was buying. And, frightening as it was, I was developing an incredible appetite for cheap scotch and boring conversation. After all, I *was* doing research. But the others—those relying on me—didn't quite see it that way. To them, I was failing. It was hell! Daily sessions of abuse from my incensed publisher . . . distraught . . . less and less sleep, more and more uptight. And, to say the least, the hype for the project was rapidly waning. The networks, the papers—all doing follow-ups. What of their offers? Had I forgotten? My world was crumbling. And *still* I hadn't found the case I needed. The case to substantiate my own importance. And then . . . I met Brad.

The STORYTELLER *crosses to the printer, rips off a few pages, and exits. Fade out. Loud, wild sax off stage. Up on* BRAD *and* LYDIA.

''S p a r & P a r r y''

BRAD *and* LYDIA *are sorting through boxes of belongings, separating what is "his" and what is "hers" into two piles.*

LYDIA: So, what was it, Brad? Huh? Great big tits? Nice long legs? What?

BRAD: That had nothing to do with it.

LYDIA: Oh no, of course not. You liked the way she picked her nose and scratched her ass in public!

He is about to put a book into his pile, she grabs it.

LYDIA: That's mine!

BRAD: It was a gift. You bought it for me.

LYDIA: You were too cheap to buy it, so I bought it. That makes it mine. *(pause)* I suppose she could put her ankles up around her head and cook breakfast at the same time?

BRAD: Don't be so crass.

LYDIA: Crass? C R A S S! Oh, that's good, Brad. That's rich! HA! Wonderful. Let's talk about refinement. Let's be civilized—YOU CHEATING FUCKING PIGHEAD . . . THESE ARE YOURS!

She hurls several beaten up work shirts at him.

BRAD: They're *yours.*

LYDIA: They are *not* mine. JEEEESUS!

BRAD: You wore them all the—

LYDIA: I don't care what I *used* to do. READ MY LIPS! I don't want them! I don't want any of it! I can't stand the sight of it. *(BRAD reaches for an old piece of driftwood)* Don't even think about it!

LYDIA *kicks it aside.*

LYDIA: You wanna paw all the wrong stuff, Brad, that's your problem. You see pretty things and your clammy little hands just reach out and touch them.

BRAD: What is this, Lydia? Suddenly everything beautiful has fallen into your hands, become yours?

LYDIA: What are you saying, Brad? What are you trying to tell me? That you are capable of recognizing beauty? You do nothing but pollute the word with your voice. If I hadn't hauled you into the world, you'd still be sitting in that musty little room, leafing through stacks of crumbling books every time you forgot how to speak. I freed you. You never would have tasted vast, open spaces—sea salt in the air . . . crashing surf.

BRAD: I'd like to keep it, if it's all the same to you.

LYDIA: I'm throwing it in the ocean. It deserves better.

BRAD: If you don't want it, I'm keeping it.

BRAD *grabs the driftwood and shoves it into a box with his other stuff.* LYDIA *pulls a fencing sword from one of the piles.*

LYDIA: This, of course, without dispute, is yours. To nurse your deflated image of the chivalrous man. To conquer whatever got in the way of your self-fulfilment, your totality. To fend off whatever was chasing you, whatever threatened you, whatever got in too close. Yeeeeesss!

She lunges at him, he steps aside.

But your weakness got the better of you, Brad. You lacked the necessary skill, the prowess needed to hold steady to the course, to succeed.

She lunges again, coming closer this time.

Instead you fell back on a blunter, cruder method of probing the

9

issue, of tearing and ploughing the flesh.

She lunges again, this time for his groin.

BRAD: HEY! Take it easy, will you!

LYDIA: You sought to conquer the world, but you failed miserably. You didn't even get past yourself! Never even touched the outside.

She places the end of the lance lightly against his chest and shoves him slowly back against the boxes.

LYDIA: What'd you go looking for, Brad? What were you after?

BRAD: I told you . . . I—

LYDIA: BULLSHIT! I WANT THE TRUTH.

BRAD: Look, you lose judgement . . . things get out of hand. It takes over—

LYDIA: WHAT DOES? WHAT TAKES OVER?

BRAD: It does! *(pause)* THE SEX!

LYDIA: THE SEX COMES LATER! Don't you remember? You meet someone first.

BRAD: Calm down will you!

LYDIA: Why? Why should I calm down? I oughta claw your eyes out. Now, for once in your *pathetic* life, let's be honest with each other. What took over?

BRAD: DESIRE . . . LUST!

LYDIA: Good. That was simple. That's all I needed to hear. It's always something simple. A tiny nugget in the stump of your brain, Brad—callin' all the shots. Every bit of willpower you ever thought you had was squashed by a microscopic, snapping neuron. Did you know that most creatures at your end of the scale don't even have spines? YOU SHOULDN'T EVEN BE ABLE TO STAND UP!

She shoves him back over the boxes.

You ran me through, Brad. I'm torn. I'm cut. I'm achin'. I'm drainin' away. All so you could feel nineteen again? I should break down and fall apart for that?

She lashes at a few boxes around him and then throws the lance to the floor.

Huh? Is that what I should throw my life away for? I think not. And you bloody well better believe it! *(pause)* You bastard!

She moves to the door.

BRAD: Lydia . . . it's the truth, I never, ever meant to hurt you.

LYDIA *stops, turns.*

LYDIA: You know what you should do, Brad? Put all this junk in a big pile and torch it. Heap it on yourself, douse it, and do the world a favour.

LYDIA *exits. The* STORYTELLER *returns.*

STORYTELLER: I began to think about what Brad had said that night in the bar. How a single event can turn your whole life upside down. It got the questions going. The theories. The idea of eternal recurrence? The will? How can I possibly influence events that are already set-up, simply waiting for me? It all comes down to one thing: survival. Doesn't matter who you are, what you do. One little thing can turn it all upside down: a phone call, a letter, someone says they saw you there. You sat at the wrong table, asked the wrong guy for a light. Something happens, outside of yourself. A thought gets tossed around in some minds, people you've never met. And suddenly, you're connected.

BETTY *crosses downstage, stops, lights a cigarette.* BRAD *crosses and turns on monitor.*

STORYTELLER: Ahhh, hindsight. Looking back to understand. The footsteps, the paths, the beauty, the shambles, the turmoil.

The STORYTELLER *moves off. Lights up on the* INFORMATIONIST's *desk.*

"The Message"

Small table, single chair, wind-up alarm clock, telephone. The INFORMATIONIST *is sitting with his feet on the table, passing time. He is leisurely playing a game of jacks (or solitaire, flipping a coin, whatever). Soft piano music accompanies the scene. This carries on long enough to be humorous. The alarm rings suddenly and loud. The* INFORMATIONIST *sits bolt-up and stares at the clock. The piano music stops. The clock rings for several seconds. He is motionless. He reaches out and turns the alarm off. He checks his watch, checks a chart, takes a deep breath and picks up the telephone receiver, dials.*

INFORMATIONIST: Love is a broken heel in the rain. *(hangs up)*

The INFORMATIONIST *resumes his game, occasionally going over his charts, schedules, checking the time.* THE SHIV *enters. He tears a page from a small notebook, tosses it on the desk, and prepares to leave.*

INFORMATIONIST: Sir?

THE SHIV: *(stopping)* Yes, Wilson?

INFORMATIONIST: I wanted to ask you . . . I've been trying to figure something out here . . .

THE SHIV: Well, what is it? What's the problem?

INFORMATIONIST: I . . . I'm just curious. I'm a bit confused about my duties, just *what* exactly it is that I do? I mean . . .

THE SHIV: Wilson, what are you talking about? You know what you are, what you do. Are you having some personal problems?

INFORMATIONIST: No, not really, I'm . . .

THE SHIV: Then what is it? You're an informationist! For god's sake, man. You relay information from the source. You are the conduit of knowledge from the outside, the missing link, the piece that brings it all together, makes it possible for us to form a discernible, coherent picture of the world. We can't have someone in such a position questioning—

INFORMATIONIST: I KNOW *WHAT* I DO!

THE SHIV: Then what's distressing you?

INFORMATIONIST: How it all fits together? What it's for? Where it goes? I mean, what's the final thing?

He grabs the ledger and randomly reads off several information bits/messages that have to be relayed.

INFORMATIONIST: "accommodate everybody's interests," "we're a damn sight closer to Newfoundland," "they come on foot, hoisting heavy sacks," "Support, not. But accept, yes—under certain circumstances." "society without the Father," "the conclusion is more than a dry inference," "modify cultural patterns," "there are absurdities not worth penetrating," "ju-jitsu," I mean, I have to know! I can't continue to sit in this room, phoning who-knows-who, at specific times, delivering obscure messages and never knowing what happens next! I speak and that's it. It ends there. I have to know how I relate to the rest of it, where I fit in! I don't think it's an odd question, sir, do you?

THE SHIV: It seems to me that doubt is implicit in your reasoning, Wilson. It may be necessary to replace you.

INFORMATIONIST: I just want to know the connection, how it works!

THE SHIV: Don't be ridiculous. You are questioning the flawless character of the authorities above you. That's unacceptable. You are given information, data—data of which, if put into the right hands, can have enormous effects on the workings of the world at large. To want to know more than that is to desire a position, a position which, by nature of its own design, would be liable to great scrutiny and eventual mistrust. You are a link in a very complex system, Wilson. I thought you understood that. To know more is harmful. For all of us. For any of us to know more than necessary is detrimental to the unit as a whole. Know the part that you play, be content with that. You *are* important. That's all you have to know. Do not doubt. Do not question what comes down from above. Accept it whole-heartedly, *implicitly*. I know no more than my position. That's all I have to know. I need to know nothing more. I want to know nothing more. Practice this philosophy, Wilson. You will be a happier and healthier man because of it. *(indicating the slip of paper)* Here, this just came in. There are other people, more powerful, more informed, who are making our decisions for us. Trust, Wilson, trust. That's all you need do. Accept everything, and question nothing.

THE SHIV *exits. The* INFORMATIONIST *rips up several 'messages' and throws them in the garbage, then burns the note* THE SHIV *brought in. The alarm clock goes off. He checks the ledger, sighs, checks his watch, reaches for the phone, then stops.*

INFORMATIONIST: GOD . . . I HATE THIS JOB!

A spot dims on him as he sits, elbows on his knees, despondent. Sax wails. STORYTELLER *enters.*

STORYTELLER: Brad became my model case. The modern man who had it all and was willing to risk it for nothing, nothing more than the experience of being *truly* alive, if only for a single moment. For once to be at the heart of an event. Something as simple as a woman on the street, standing in the rain, flagging cabs. No one will touch her, you offer her a ride. The dominoes begin to fall. Someone says they've seen you in Chinatown, always after the bars close, always alone. Something happens, outside of you. People want to know who you are, what you're about. Someone else in another part of town feels uneasy, they're nervous. Certain connections are bad, they spell trouble. Who's right? Who's telling the story and what's at stake? That's the issue. There's a reality out there somewhere. It's there, and then it's gone. And what's left? People, bits of data, and someone who wants to make connections.

The STORYTELLER *exits.*

SCENE III

"Chinatown"

Lights up on FAT MAN's *apartment.* JIMMY *is sitting at the table toying with a syringe. He is taking water up into it, flicking the bubbles to the top, and then spraying the contents out onto his pant leg. He repeats this procedure over and over.*

FAT MAN *enters whistling "It's A Long Way To Tipperary". He is carrying a wad of bills. As he speaks he flips through the bundle of money.*

FAT MAN: "It's a long, long way to Tipperary. It's a l-o-n-g way to Hell." I tell you, Jim. That's what it's gonna be when I bust that prick—HELL! He's gonna wish he never started this shit. The stupid fuck!

JIMMY: What're we gonna do? Nobody's buyin'.

FAT MAN: You think I don't know that? Why don't you tell me something I don't know for a change? I can't exist on this. I'm losin' a fuckin' grand a day while that pimp plays Mr. Big Guy. Yeah, sure. Payin' top dollar, and droppin' it at three-cut prices. Just to fuck my head. *(pause)* Well, I'll tell you somethin', Jim. I don't like it. Not a bit. All this does, these kinda stupid tactics, is cause inflation. Inflates the whole fuckin' economy, presents a false sense of *urgency* to our *clientele*. And for what? That's my question. What purpose does this serve?

JIMMY: We could just dump the stuff and go back to sellin' pot?

FAT MAN: What did you say?

JIMMY: It's crazy! Just dump it. We're just sittin' on this stuff and

15

nobody's buyin'—

FAT MAN: WILL YOU STOP SAYIN' THAT! I am well aware that nobody's buyin'.

JIMMY: It was just easier then, that's all.

FAT MAN: Go back to sellin' *pot*? Jesus . . . you fuckin' loser. Don't you see what he's doin'? Don't you get it? He's tryin' to scare us out, but I don't run from no one. This guy bites his own nose in spite of his dog-puke face. Best brown to come into this city in years . . . and enough demand for both of us. I mean, what sort of stupid sense does this *make*?

JIMMY: Asshole sense.

FAT MAN: EXACTLY! We're stuck with this sub-standard shit while he burns his profit and slits my throat at the same time. It's nuts!

JIMMY: All I know is I haven't had a thing to eat in three days, there's stuff all around me, and I can't even have a hit! I'm just sayin' that we did all right before. We didn't have to deal with this sort of bullshit.

FAT MAN: Listen, asshole. You wanna go get somethin' to eat, there's the door. You wanna drag your ass all over town sellin' dimebags—then go ahead. I'm not backin' out now. He wants to fuck with me, then let him. It's only a matter of time before the situation breaks. Old . . . Man . . . Time. We just *sit* and *wait*, we stick it out 'til the situation breaks. *(pause)* And it always does. It always breaks.

The phone rings. JIMMY *picks it up fast,* FAT MAN *grabs it out of his hand.* BETTY *is calling from the* INFORMATIONIST's *desk.*

FAT MAN: Yeah.

BETTY: Arnie? It's Betty. How's it goin'?

FAT MAN: Do I know you?

BETTY: Sure . . . you know me. Well, we're acquaintances actually, but I always felt there was more to it than that.

FAT MAN: Hold on a sec. Jimmy! Some broad named Betty. Says she knows me. We know a Betty?

JIMMY *doesn't respond, keeps playing with the syringe.* FAT MAN *shoves him from behind.*

Shit-fer-brains, I'm talkin' to you!

JIMMY: *(jumping to his feet)* Fuck's sake, what're you doin'?

FAT MAN: Askin' a fuckin' question, that's what. I got a lady on the line, I'm tryin' to put a face to a name. All right? Help out a little—

JIMMY: You don't shove somebody when they're holdin' a spike! All right? Where's your fuckin' brains?

FAT MAN: *(into the phone)* Hang on, I'll be right with you. *(back to* JIMMY*)* Asshole, there is a sexy voice on this phone . . . she knows me, my real name. So, I turn to my partner—who, I might add, so anxiously grabbed the phone—hoping for a little assistance, but he's spellbound by a dimestore plunger. Fuck! If it's not too much to ask, asshole, help out a bit! *(he kicks* JIMMY's *chair, returns to phone)* Sorry. One of those days . . . How 'bout a little hint as to where I was graced by your company. The voice is vaguely . . .

JIMMY: Leo.

FAT MAN: . . . familiar . . . but you know how it is, we meet so many people.

JIMMY: Leo's Betty. She spanned your pupils for days. It was disgusting. You swore you were gonna fast 'til you dropped sixty pounds. What a joke.

FAT MAN: Hold on a sec' . . . *(to* JIMMY*)* How many times have I told you? Huh! It's fucking-near impossible to listen to your chatter and make sense of a phone call at the same time. All right?

JIMMY: Leo!

FAT MAN: Leo what? Leo, Leo, Leo! What the fuck are you talkin' about?

JIMMY: LEO! The asshole who's puttin' us out of business. His ole lady . . . .

FAT MAN: Betty. Shiiiit. I apologize. Got so much on my goddamn mind I can't even think straight. Why your voice did not trigger an immediate vision and a pounding heartbeat shall forever remain a mystery. How you doin'?

BETTY: Never been better. I want to talk to you about something.

FAT MAN: Like what?

BETTY: A proposition. One involving very large amounts of money.

FAT MAN: Really. Well . . . that may not be the sort of thing we should be discussin' over the lines. I mean, it would be so much more civilized to have you drop by . . . you know . . . in the flesh. The deadness of these machines just doesn't do you justice. We've become strangers to ourselves . . . aliens . . . our primitive, tribal urges have been lost . . . we distrust one another . . . like animals.

BETTY: Ok. I'll come over. I'll see you in twenty minutes.

BETTY *hangs up.* FAT MAN *is stunned. He visibly inflates at the thought of* BETTY's *presence. He drops the receiver to the floor and grabs* JIMMY *by the front of the shirt.*

FAT MAN: She's coming over! Here! NOW! SHE'S GONNA BE IN THIS ROOM! TODAY! IN TWENTY MINUTES! DO YOU HEAR ME!? ARE YOU BREATHING? ARE YOU STILL ALIVE? TWEEEEENTYYYYY MINNNNNUTES!

While FAT MAN *has been carrying on,* JIMMY *has doused the crotch of* FAT MAN's *jeans with a syringe-ful of water.*

JIMMY: HEY! HOLD IT! HOLD IT! *(he calms* FAT MAN *slightly)* You pissed yourself. You got so goddamned excited, you pissed yourself.

FAT MAN *staggers back a few steps, looking down in disbelief.* JIMMY *starts laughing and pointing, holding the syringe up as the lights dim.*

FAT MAN: I'll get ya' for that, James. I will. I promise. I'll get ya'.

FAT MAN *walks off to a corner, counting his cash and whistling "Tipperary". Lights up on* BRAD *at the* INFORMATIONIST's *desk.*

''The Interrogation''

The monitor snaps on with a news broadcast. A female announcer reading the news.

MONITOR: Three people were killed yesterday in what appears to have been a battle over drug territory. Dead are Arnold Raymond Johnson of Surrey; Leonard Wiltshire of Vancouver; Staff Sgt. Mark Donnelly of the Vancouver Vice Squad; also found at the scene was James Duprez, of no fixed address, an apparent victim of a heroin overdose. A suspect has been apprehended, and is being held for questioning.

The monitor goes to snow. Enter THE SHIV.

THE SHIV: OK. You pick her up in your car, she's waiting at the corner, where I presume you arranged to meet. You cruise off for a leisurely roundabout, then you park down at the docks and make it in your car like a couple of teenagers. Exciting maybe, but not very discreet. That part's fine, not at all out of character for the woman in question, but what does not follow is why you? What did she need from you that she couldn't get from a dozen other crooked CA's in town with more money and far better looks? That's what doesn't figure, Brad. That's what we're havin' a bit of a time with. That's what the good doctor and I are here for. That's when we get called in, when things don't figure. Science and tact, we're here.

The monitor snaps back to the news broadcast.

MONITOR: Staff Sgt. Donnelly, who it is believed had inside information regarding a major payoff between the two rivals, was welcomed at the scene with rapid gunfire. A witness at the Carl Rooms commented that "it was just like the movies, only more real."

BRAD *is handcuffed to a chair centre stage, next to the* INFORMATIONIST's *desk. On the desk is the alarm clock. He is being questioned by* THE SHIV *and* DR. MARTIN *over a P.A. system from opposite sides of the room. The video monitor is on, no picture, just snow on the screen.*

THE SHIV: Bradley? Can you hear me?

BRAD: Yes.

THE SHIV: Good. We'll proceed.

BRAD: I wanna know why I'm being held here?

THE SHIV: Brad, we'd like to ask you a couple of questions. We have complete knowledge of your background, what you do, who you are, so please don't waste time dwelling on that. Just the facts.

BRAD: Look, you drag me down here, no explanation—I just want to know what's going—

THE SHIV: Good, then we're here for one and the same purpose. We'll move through this as quickly as possible.

BRAD: You can't just hold me here! What do you think I've done?

THE SHIV: We need some information.

BRAD: Fine, ok. I kinda gathered that. Didn't think you invited me down here for lunch. It's just a bit extreme, don't you think? *(pause)* I mean, I'm willing to co-operate, I'll help you out if I can. But I'm not a criminal, you know that. Are you there? HEY! Whadya want? Whadya need to know? I want out of here. Come on! Can you hear me? Let's get on with it!

THE SHIV: Wasting time, Brad. Sitting around wasting time as if we had idle moments to fill with brainless, smartass jokes. I don't need it. I do not have time for useless information in my day. I do not have *idle moments*. I need substance every step of the way, discussion that changes the course of things, that has an effect.

That is why they call me The Shiv, Brad. I'm fast, efficient, and to the point. I get the job done in record time and with the least amount of misery. Now, *may we resume?*

BRAD: Yes. *(pause)* I'm sorry.

THE SHIV: Tell me about the girl.

BRAD: What girl? Who?

THE SHIV: The girl in the pouring rain. You picked her up.

BRAD: I don't know what the hell you're talking about.

DR. MARTIN: I think you're lying, Brad.

BRAD: *(snapping around)* Who's that?

THE SHIV: That is Doctor Martin.

BRAD: Doctor?

THE SHIV: That's right. A forensic psychologist. We work together—on occasion.

BRAD: This is insane! If you know my past then you know you've got the wrong guy. I can't be this important. I'm an accountant for chrissake!

THE SHIV: We understand you're way out of your league with this one. You've been known to doctor up a pretty good audit, and once came shockingly close to being brought up on embezzlement charges—unreported revenue I believe, ah . . . August, 1985—but you were smart enough to sock it away in equity funds under the company name.

DR. MARTIN: Very common for those heading into their mid-thirties. Identity Crisis. High-need achiever with a low batting average, frantic to leave his mark.

THE SHIV: That little incident took a few years off your life, but not particularly relevant to this case. Thing is, Brad, we're having a bit of a tough time making the connections on this one. That's where you can help us out.

BRAD: I'm dreaming! This isn't real. I'm dead! I passed out

somewhere and fuckin'-well died!

DR. MARTIN: You seem nervous, Brad.

BRAD: Of course I'm nervous! I just don't get what's—AHHHH!

An extremely loud alarm bell/buzzer goes off. BRAD lurches wildly in his seat. The alarm goes on for several seconds. The monitor comes on with a scene of several people getting busted. THE SHIV and DR. MARTIN enter. The monitor goes to snow. THE SHIV and DR. MARTIN move off stage.

BRAD: What the hell's going on? I want to speak to a lawyer! This is harassment! You hear me?

The monitor clicks on. BRAD is on the monitor speaking to BRAD at the desk. Monitor Brad is smoking a cigar.

MONITOR: Oh, man, I get so tired. New things to learn . . . ideas . . . up and down, everything changing. I mean, I get worn out just *thinkin'* about keepin' up.

BRAD: What're you talkin' about? Keepin' up with what? With who? These guys? You know what's goin' on?

MONITOR: Oh, yeah, it's easy. You got nothin' to worry about. Little bit of information in the wrong hands, got a few people worked up. Couple of guys are dead, a cop's dead, pretty everyday stuff. Hell, what's all the flap about? Relaaaax. Have a scotch.

BRAD: I don't want a goddamn scotch! I want the hell out of here. Gimme some information, something I can work with. You're not giving me anything to go on.

MONITOR: Weeell, that's just the nature of my being. I'm not threatening, I don't challenge anything you believe in, but I am loyal company in times of need.

BRAD: I made a phone call.

MONITOR: Yeah, shit, I've made that mistake before. You never know what the hell you're gonna say when you get on one of those things.

BRAD: THIS IS SERIOUS! They think I'm involved with this other stuff, this woman—drugs, money . . .

MONITOR: Then rearrange the facts, man. It's your history. Tell them
a different story, make it believable, toss in some details to spice it
up, twist it around, give it some depth. Make them buy it. Make *it*
the truth. Just *listen* to them. They got some screwball scenario,
they're linkin' up dots, creatin' an image—a picture is taking form.
And you, my boy, are at the centre of it. Or, just lay back and let
the experience wash over you like a warm wave of loooove.

BRAD: What're you talkin' about? A picture of what? Of who? I
haven't done anything. I'm innocent!

MONITOR: Yeah, sure, we're all innocent. Tell them that. They've
heard it a million times. You got two guys there with a need, that
much is easy to see. Find out what the picture is, man, and give it
to them, give them what they want. You sure you don't want that
scotch? Man, this is some cigar.

Monitor BRAD *reclines and blows a long cloud of smoke. Screen goes to*
snow.

BRAD: HEY!!! Hey, wait! Gimme more! I gotta have more to go on.

THE SHIV: Brad?

BRAD: STAY WITH ME! DON'T GO!

DR. MARTIN: Are you all right, Brad? *(pause)* BRADLEY?

BRAD: OH, JESUS, HELP ME. I'M TALKIN' TO THE GODDAMN T.V.!

THE SHIV: Time's up, Brad.

BRAD: WHADYA MEAN, TIME'S UP?

DR. MARTIN: Love is a broken heel in the rain.

THE SHIV: What did she mean, Brad?

DR. MARTIN: Love . . . is a broken heel . . . in the rain.

BRAD: What do you mean? What are you talkin' about.

DR. MARTIN: We're talking about pictures, Brad. Pictures of you and
a particular woman.

An overhead projector snaps on and projects a series of shots of BRAD *and* BETTY *on the street, talking, getting into* BRAD's *car.*

DR. MARTIN: Our staff Sergeant was well aware of who the woman in the picture was. He knew what the tip was trying to say. Two days later he received a call. He was told to listen to the Informer's Line—Wednesday, 5:15. He knew what he'd be listening for. If it was there, that was a "go", mobilization, action. That's how things work down here. But against police procedure, he took no backup. Something else was at stake. That's what we think you know. We need that information!

THE SHIV: Simple, Brad. That's all we have to know. The meaning. Give it to us and you're free to go. Tell us! What was the point of the phrase? Tell us what she meant!

BRAD *turns and leans over his shoulder, facing the monitor. The lights dim slightly. A mournful saxophone wails behind.*

"The Weakness"

Lights up on FAT MAN's *apartment.* FAT MAN *is primping himself, putting on after shave etc.* JIMMY *sits at the table, smoking.*

FAT MAN: Come on, straighten the place up a bit.

JIMMY: Why? So you can mess it up again? It ain't worth it.

FAT MAN: You asshole. Want her to think we're a couple of slobs? Come on, have a bit of class.

FAT MAN *rushes around tidying up,* JIMMY *picks up the ashtrays and is about to go empty them.)*

JIMMY: If you had any *class,* you'd use her to get that bastard.

FAT MAN: How so?

JIMMY: Nobody knows him better than her. You get the woman, you get the man. Dig?

FAT MAN: You know, James, sometimes you say the most *incredible* things. Visions! Insights! *Real ideas!* But it is so seldom, that I forget why I keep you around. YES! Of course. Through the woman . . . to the man.

BETTY *enters.*

FAT MAN: Speaking of visions . . .

BETTY: Don't clean up on my account, Jim.

JIMMY: Just doin' my bit, you know. Getcha beer . . . ?

BETTY: No . . . I'm fine. Thanks.

FAT MAN: I do say . . . nicest thing I've seen in months. Hey, Jim, why don't you go to the store and get us some smokes.

JIMMY: 'Cause I hate stores.

FAT MAN: Come on, give us a few minutes alone—

BETTY: Jim's not a problem. There's no big secret here. We all know each other. So, how're things?

FAT MAN: Excellent. Business is booming.

BETTY: Is that so? That's not what I hear.

FAT MAN: Oh? And what do you hear?

BETTY: I hear that Leo's wiping you out, that he plans on makin' you extinct.

FAT MAN: Is that a fact.

BETTY: Yeah. I also hear that you're sittin' on a pile of garbage that you'd be lucky to drop for cost.

FAT MAN: And where'd you hear that?

BETTY: Oh, just people, Arnie. I *talk* to people. I *know* people. I listen to what they say.

FAT MAN: I'm sure you do. He may be chippin' at my profit margin, but that's about it.

BETTY: So, what do you plan on doin'?

FAT MAN: I thought you came by to talk business? Leo send you over to see how I'm makin' out? Is that it? Huh? Is that your *business*, Betty? Well, tell Leo I'm fine! Just fine! You tell your dumb-ass old man that.

BETTY: He didn't send me, Arnie. We're not even an item anymore. We're history.

FAT MAN: Oh, really? I didn't know that. I'm sorry to hear it.

JIMMY: Oh, shit. *(gets up to leave)* Two packs?

FAT MAN: Carton.

JIMMY *exits.*

BETTY: I am here on business. Half of what Leo has should be mine. I got fuck-all from him. Dumped. Four years and I'm left with nothing. I refuse to deal with him anymore.

FAT MAN: Well, at least we have *something* in common.

BETTY: I got an idea, an idea that can land us a fast twenty grand. And if I can burn Leo in the process, all the sweeter.

FAT MAN: That's not something you pull just because you're pissed off at somebody.

BETTY: I've thought it out, don't worry. Listen, Arnie, I did a lot for that man. Running, all sorts of shit, and I got nothing to show for it. Everything was always tied up—here, there . . . always one day . . . one day, baby, we're gonna be rich! We'll live like Kings! Yeah, right. Now I'm on the street without a dollar to my name.

FAT MAN: You're welcome to stay here—if you need a place.

BETTY: I can't take him myself, Arnie. That's the whole thing. But together, we can do it. We can shaft that bastard good.

FAT MAN: Yeah?

BETTY: Look . . . just listen to me, see what you think. I pressure him for, say ten, twenty-thou. Short-term loan, to get me on my feet. What choice has he got? I could lead the cops to half a dozen safety deposit boxes tomorrow. We take what he fronts me, and undercut his prices. We pull the people—the regulars—back to you, break down the power. Leo's out of the way. We got the clientele and we take it from there.

FAT MAN: Of course you know this is madness? You think Leo's just gonna stand by and watch his life turn to shit?

BETTY: I don't care what he does. In two months he's gonna break everybody anyway. We make a move now or pack it in.

FAT MAN: Ok. Ok. You got a point there, I know. I've just been tryin' to avoid this sort of crap.

BETTY: Once he's out of the way, it'll be you and me. We'll be the ones callin' the shots.

FAT MAN: Hmmmm . . . I like the sound of that.

FAT MAN moves over to BETTY. She puts her arm around his neck, gives him a kiss on the cheek.

BETTY: A lot of people are very pissed off at Leo, you for one. The word's out. It's not good business. This environment draws the heat, creates tension. It's good for nobody. People get nervous, people get hurt. It's gotta end. We'll be set. Happy customers, good business . . . that can buy a lot of silence, if you know what I mean.

FAT MAN: Yeah . . . I hear what you're sayin'. Just you and me.

BETTY: You got it. And more money than we'll know what to do with.

FAT MAN: Ya' know, Betty . . . I like a lady with brains.

BETTY: Then you're gonna *love* me. Now, this is how I say we work it . . . .

The lights dim on FAT MAN and BETTY. Soft piano interlude.

"The Connection"

Lights up downstage right. BETTY *enters and moves downstage right,* BRAD *follows. Sound of rain.*

BETTY: You shouldn't have said anything!

BRAD: Why not?

BETTY: Because it's none of your business.

BRAD: I didn't like the way he was talking to you.

BETTY: What d'you know about it? I told you to move, you should have left.

BRAD: The guy's an asshole!

BETTY: Listen, you don't know who you're dealing with. Ok?

BRAD: Well, who is he?

BETTY: Is that any of your business?

BRAD: Hey, come on . . . we were gettin' along, havin' fun weren't we?

BETTY: We live together—*lived* together. He kicked me out. Does that clear things up? Now, please, just *get lost!*

BRAD: Hey, I'm sorry . . . I'll walk with you.

BETTY: I'm going home! Christ, what does it take?

BRAD: I'll give you a ride.

BETTY: What is this? All of a sudden I got a guardian angel?

BRAD: I'm just offering . . . as a favour.

BETTY: Shouldn't you be getting home to your *wife?*

BRAD: Who said I'm married?

BETTY: No one. You just look married. You act like you *belong* to someone.

BRAD: Noooo.

BETTY: Is that what you call it?

BRAD: What?

BETTY: Driving me home, trying to bed me . . . that's doing me a favour?

BRAD: I . . . I never said anything about—

BETTY: *(turning on him)* You wanna do me a favour, a real simple favour?

BRAD: Anything. Just name it . . . but can we get out of the rain, can we just get in the car?

BETTY: *(digging in her purse, then)* Read this.

BRAD: Why? What is it?

BETTY: Just read it.

BRAD: "Love is . . . a . . . " I can't make it out.

BETTY: READ IT!

BRAD: Hey, relax. I'm trying, ok? It's all wet, it's soaked. Look at it.

BETTY: Just say it, out loud.

BRAD: "Love is a . . . bro . . . bro—"

BETTY: LOUDER!

BRAD: "Love is a . . . broken . . . " I . . . I can't—just tell me.

BETTY: It's a poem, my poem!

BRAD: A poem?

BETTY: Yeah, a new one, it's the first line. A *broken heel* . . . in the rain. SAY IT!

BRAD: *(they chant in unison)* 'Love is a broken heel in the rain.' Not very optimistic.

BETTY: It's as true as any line about love, don't you think? And it would mean a lot to me if you'd phone a certain number on a certain day and recite that line. Would you do that for me? Just say it and hang up. My line, my poem. A simple favour for a friend. And to express my appreciation, I'll give you a thousand dollars. Ten, crisp, one-hundred dollar bills.

BRAD: A thousand bucks! For what?

BETTY: To make it worth your while, to make sure you don't forget. Because it means a lot to me. It'll be something to remember me by.

BRAD: Remember you?

BETTY: Yes . . . this bar, my poem, this night! *(she kisses him)* Say you'll do it and I'll take that ride home. *(kisses him again)* And maybe that drink, too. *(They get into BRAD's car)*

THE SHIV *and* DR. MARTIN *enter and move to the interrogation area and begin reviewing the slides of* BRAD *and* BETTY.

THE SHIV: We've got bugger-all to go on. *(1st slide shows BETTY and BRAD standing by BRAD's car)* The kid's clean. He hasn't done a thing.

DR. MARTIN: You're approaching the situation with the wrong attitude, Ken.

THE SHIV: Am I? *(slide #2 on screen: BETTY and BRAD kissing passionately)*

DR. MARTIN: I'm afraid so. These are not simply pictures that we're looking at. They're pieces of lives, events that now form a part of a collective past. Shards, Ken. Like a broken mirror, or an old faded photograph of Hitler patting young children on the head. Pieces of a larger picture. It takes a fine eye to discern the reality. Illusions, shrouds, masking other elements which are now hidden from sight. We must drive ourselves to speculate. We must ask ourselves what can be implied?

THE SHIV: Yeeeees, I see.

DR. MARTIN: He's connected, but how? *(slide #3: in the car, parked)* The question is not "if", but "how". How do we get him to reveal the big picture?

THE SHIV: Absolutely . . . yes. And between the two of us, I'm sure we can figure that out.

"The Need"

Lights crossover to BETTY *and* LEO, *upstage right.* LEO *is in a chair, weighing out packets on a set of scales.*

BETTY: How many times did I cover for you? Huh? You wouldn't be who you are today if it wasn't for me.

LEO: You're right, I'd be a much richer man.

BETTY: Fuck you, Leo!

LEO: Is that any way to ask a friend for a favour?

BETTY: I'm not asking for favours, Leo. I'm askin' for what's due me, that's all. For the time I put in. What did I get? Tossed over for some scrawny ditchpig? You owe me, Leo.

LEO: I owe you nothing! You liked spending money, and we did. Lots of it. You're free now, so go spend somebody else's. It's not my problem.

BETTY: You are such a prick sometimes. You give nothing. All I'm askin' for is a bit of backing. One week. Just long enough to turn it around.

LEO: I don't know, maybe I'm stupid, but it seems to me that someone asking for that kind of money would be just a little more . . . polite? *(he turns, wraps his arm around her thigh, and pulls her closer)* If you know what I mean?

BETTY: Yeah, I see what you mean. I'm outa here. *(she starts to go)*

LEO: You're takin' it all wrong. It could be good. Best of friends. Do what we want, when we want. It's just sometimes . . . I get this uncontrollable desire to—

BETTY: Where's your *girlfriend*, Leo? School? Walk out already? You don't toss people away like an old pair of shoes, and expect them to be there when you need them. It doesn't work that way.

LEO: This is different!

BETTY: Is it?

LEO: YES! It's not some deal you make—just an exchange of goods. This is us, our life. Just because we're not sleeping together doesn't mean it's over. The situation's always changing.

BETTY: What are you saying, Leo? It's different now?

LEO: I just want us to be friends, to stay close. Personally, and in business. Why go somewhere else? I got the best stuff in town right here. You know that.

BETTY: Because I'd still be relying on you. Don't you see? I can't do that anymore. I gotta make it on my own. And if it's handled right, we'll both come out ahead.

LEO: What's in it for me?

BETTY: Trust me, Leo. You'll get your money back and more. It'll put me on my feet, and you'll be number one in the city.

LEO: I'm number one now!

BETTY: Well, yeah.

LEO: Whadya mean, well, yeah. Who the fuck you think's bigger than me? Huh? Ohhh . . . Fat Man. You're dealin' with that pig? Is that it? Speak up, Betty. You're not comin' through, you're not makin' sense. Let's be up front here, shall we?

BETTY: Ok. Yeah, you're right. I'm gonna take him.

LEO: What're you talkin' about? On your own? You're fuckin' dreamin'.

BETTY: You watch. I'm gonna do it.

LEO: Don't be so stupid.

BETTY: But I need the money. I owe people, remember?

LEO: Then borrow it for that and forget this other shit.

BETTY: Back me for thirty. I can *do it*. I know I can, Leo. He'll front me an ounce for thirty. One week. That's it. I'll dump it fast and have your money back in a week, ten days at the most. *(pause)* Look, all I do is tell him I want two. When I show up I tell him there's problems, things didn't pan out how I expected, I could only pull together enough for one. Now he's set up on the drop. He's sittin' pretty with thirty G's and at least another ounce on his person. Once I'm out, you move in with a couple of guys—

LEO: HEY! WAIT A SECOND! Hold it! Hold it. *Me* and a couple of guys?

BETTY: It'll work! It's simple. I get an ounce, you get an ounce, and Fat Man's on the street. I just thought . . .

LEO: I do not believe the shit I'm hearing. What'd you do, come up with this over breakfast? Why in hell do I want my name involved in this? Huh? I don't like it. You're lookin' for an easy way out, fast money. And if this is the best you can come up with, you better go back to waitressing.

BETTY: What are you sayin', Leo. You won't back me?

LEO: That's right, that's what I'm sayin'.

BETTY: OK. Fine. Just fine. Just fuck you, Leo! I don't believe this! I ask you—as a friend—that's all. As a friend, for one week.

LEO: I'll tell you something, Betty. You got no tact, no class. You got a lot to learn about protocol, dealing with people. 'Cause you're goin' nowhere but down—fast!

BETTY: What do I have to do, beg you? Is that it? You wanna belittle me some more? Play the big kingpin? Just front me the *money!*

LEO: It's too *risky!* He gets onto this, takes the thirty, slaps you around, and that's the end of it. Where will you be then? Huh? That's all I'm sayin'. Think about it.

BETTY: RISK? You are something else! You wanna talk about risk? How many times did I risk my life, risk going away? Huh? The decoy, the bait, the drop-off—all your small con shit! How many times, Leo?

LEO: I'm the one who'll be out thirty grand, not you. Am I right?

BETTY: You bastard. *(pause)* Friends? You wanna be friends? You don't know what that *is*, Leo. Where's the trust, the loyalty? Huh? You'd let me go down, out on the street? Does that sound like a friend? *(pause)* So just say it. One way or the other. You make the decision. Right now. You know how to do that, you're good at it.

LEO stands, leans BETTY back over the table, kisses her hard.

LEO: You're trouble, you know that? One goddamn bitch of trouble.

BETTY: The best. And you'll help me, I know it.

LEO: You've always been trouble. It never stops.

BETTY: Never. You'll help me save myself.

They kiss again, harder, more vicious.

LEO: You'll always be trouble . . . always.

BETTY: YES! Oh, yes . . . yes . . .

LEO: You'll destroy me yet, I know it.

They continue kissing, roughly.

BETTY: YES! YES!

They gradually move up on the table as the lights dim. Piano interlude accompanies the STORYTELLER as he moves slowly out from upstage right. He stands near the table, and observes BETTY and LEO as they begin to writhe and 'devour' each other. The STORYTELLER lights a cigarette.

"Picture Forming"

STORYTELLER: Something happens, outside of yourself. A thought gets tossed around in some minds . . . suddenly, you're connected.

He moves over toward centre stage, near the monitor. The lights go down on BETTY *and* LEO. *The monitor snaps on, only snow.* BRAD *is once again cuffed to the chair; he has been badly beaten.* THE SHIV *enters and crosses to* BRAD.

BRAD: I don't know the connection! I don't know what you want!

THE SHIV: We've got *pictures*, a *tape* . . . we've got a case.

BRAD: I don't know anything. I've told you that, over and over.

STORYTELLER: Information out of control. Clarity breaking down.

BRAD: I made a phone call, that's it.

THE SHIV: MUST WE GO THROUGH THIS AGAIN? *(he slaps* BRAD*)*

STORYTELLER: Fascinating! In this day and age, a man willing to die for an idea, the idea of innocence.

BRAD: *(to* THE SHIV*)* I wanted some adventure, that's all!

THE SHIV: OK! Finally we're getting somewhere.

STORYTELLER: Billions of pieces of data—manipulated, tampered with, acted upon.

The lights dim. The other characters are visible in the periphery. A spot comes up above BRAD.

BRAD: It was a chance to run in another life and return unscathed?

Yes. The scent of freedom. As a child I had a dream. I saw my father and I saw that he was trapped, trapped inside his own life. With no way out. And he was crying, crying for things I did not yet know, for all the things he would never be able to protect me from. He knew that I, too, would one day encounter things with a weight too heavy to bear. I woke up running.

STORYTELLER: Survival, remember? Yeah, that's what it's all about.

BETTY *enters from upstage left, encircling* BRAD.

BETTY: *(she picks up the phone)* YOU WERE RIGHT! HE SLAPPED ME AROUND AND THREW ME OUT! YES! HE'S GOT THE MONEY, ALL OF IT! I'M SORRY, LEO. I'M SORRY! *(she pretends to be crying, hangs up the phone, laughs wildly. The* VICE CAPTAIN *enters)* It's all set up. I'll leave the message, the first line of my poem, the one I read to you last night. That'll be the go-ahead.

VICE CAPTAIN: You're brilliant, simply *brilliant.*

BETTY: Ohhh, but the pictures, the tape, they're perfect! *(they kiss)* Both of them together . . . we'll squash them like bugs. *(they kiss again)* We're going to be rich! FILTHY RICH!

THE SHIV: We need answers on this one, Brad. We're talking triple-homicide. A simple conviction as an accessory will get you five to ten. Isn't it time you told us what you know?

STORYTELLER: It was my fear of intimacy holding me back. An intimacy with the world. I had to decide. Surrender, or hold back? The decision was mine. It was a theory of *passion*, the passion to evolve. How to give back to the world what I'd taken. How to surrender.

BRAD: I did someone a favour, that's all. I'm innocent. I can't be blamed for things I know nothing about!

STORYTELLER: And that's exactly what was about to happen.

THE SHIV: OK. You pick the girl up, right? *(pause)* RIGHT? That *is you* in the picture. Correct? So, you stop, you pick up the girl, yes?

BRAD: *(pause)* Yes.

THE SHIV: She gives you instructions regarding a message. Something to do with Sergeant Donnelly, a major drug transaction. Correct?

BRAD *doesn't respond.* THE SHIV *takes a cassette tape off the table, shoves it into the tape player. It plays:*

> BETTY: 'On a specific day, at a specific time, you'll call a number, say the line, and hang up. That's all. Just say it and hang up. It's worth a grand.'

> BRAD: 'No problem. Will you need me for backup?'

> BETTY: 'Not at this point. You'll get the other thousand when it's all over.'

BRAD: THAT'S NOT WHAT I SAID!

BETTY *enters upstage, crosses to the interrogation area.*

BETTY: Yes, Bradley, be straight with them. Tell them everything. You were straight with me, straight up and hard. *(she laughs hysterically)*

THE SHIV: She gave you instructions regarding the message. You agreed to do it for a fee. Right?

BRAD: That's not my voice! It's a lie!

THE SHIV: What did the message mean?

BRAD: I TOLD YOU, I DON'T KNOW!

THE SHIV: Why ask about 'backup'? For who? Where?

BRAD: THAT'S NOT ME ON THE TAPE!

THE SHIV: It sounds like your voice to me! Brad, I think you fail to see the seriousness of your situation. Sergeant Donnelly is dead! The pieces of this mixed up mess all seem to point to you.

BETTY: Such a sweet kid, just in the wrong place at the right time. *(exits)*

THE SHIV: *(to himself)* I'm so tired of this. The end of my day, end of my week, and this is what I get. Static, white noise, no communication. *(to* BRAD*)* You meet the girl, you get the money! What's the connection? *(he lights a cigarette and crosses D.S. The slides come back on behind* BRAD*)*

The monitor snaps on to the image of BRAD. BRAD *slowly comes to.*

MONITOR: People never listen. They take me for granted! I hate that! They just don't listen! I lay it out, clear as can be, but they insist on complicating things. Be pragmatic, stick to the facts!

BRAD: They believe nothing. A simple phone call . . . I lie, I tell the truth—

MONITOR: Because you obscure everything! Now they'll believe nothing but themselves, only their own hopeless sense of reason!

BRAD: 'Love is a broken heel in the rain' . . . I know nothing . . . I know everything.

MONITOR: Man, I need a drink! I gotta get a drink! *(pulls out a cigar)* Who's got a light? You got a match? DOES ANYONE HAVE A LIGHT!

The STORYTELLER *fiddles with the monitor, and once again gets the shot of the fire.* BRAD *slips from consciousness.*

STORYTELLER: Forever a case of being on your guard. A new show every time you go out there. He had information, held it in confidence, then turned it loose. He thought it meant nothing, that it had no power. He was isolated. Inside a box with road-map walls. And late in the night of each day Brad tried to figure out where to turn the course so it would never cross the other lines again. *(pause)* He was charting his own death. *(He turns, warms his hands.)* Ahhh, that's better. Damn cold on the outside.

The STORYTELLER *warms his hands for a few moments, lights a cigarette, and wanders off. The lights dim. Only the monitor, the flames, and* BRAD. *A very dim light comes up on* JIMMY *and* FAT MAN's *apartment.* JIMMY *is face-down on the table,* FAT MAN *is pacing around. He has a long knife tucked in the back of his belt. He keeps checking his watch, looking out the window, listening by the door. The remainder of this sequence moves in a very slow, dream-like quality.* LEO *enters. No words are spoken.* LEO *and* FAT MAN *acknowledge each other. They circle slowly around the table where* JIMMY *sits, eyeing each other all the time. After several times around the table, alternating directions,* FAT MAN *stops and turns, waits for* LEO *to advance.* LEO *stops, they stare. They nod to one another, and* LEO *advances, slowly.* FAT MAN *draws his blade, holds it at his side. As they move closer,* LEO *reaches inside his jacket for a revolver.* BRAD *starts to mumble incoherently. He is dreaming, caught in a nightmare.* FAT MAN *lunges as* LEO *pulls his revolver out.* LEO *gets it in the stomach just as the* VICE CAPTAIN *appears in the doorway, pistol drawn. He takes aim on the* FAT MAN *and fires.* FAT MAN *crashes across the table and slides to the floor.* LEO *has rolled over, he is barely coherent. He tries to pull himself toward the door.* BETTY *enters and moves toward the* VICE CAPTAIN. *They embrace, kiss quickly. She turns away.* BETTY *picks up the money, some drugs, opens her purse and crams it full. She pulls a revolver, turns, and plugs the* VICE CAPTAIN.

She goes to LEO, *who is moaning, dying on the floor. She holds his head to her chest for a few moments, then exits quickly.* BRAD *is starting to thrash and scream, trying to awake. The alarm beside* BRAD *goes off. He snaps bolt upright, yelling in terror. The monitor flickers with flames. The lights on* FAT MAN *and the rest snap off.*

BRAD: NO! NO! NNNNNOOOOOO!

The monitor comes on and begins to replay scenes of the murders. Several angles, with slight variations, are shown. A spot comes up on BRAD. *He's confused. He looks around, tries to calm himself, then returns to the monitor, transfixed by the images. The replay sequence continues as the lights come down on the monitor area.*

BRAD *and* LYDIA *enter and move downstage. They are wearing heavy winter coats or sweaters. They are out strolling.*

LYDIA: I've given it a lot of thought and I've decided to quit my job, make a move.

BRAD: What . . . why?

LYDIA: It's become too much. The gossip, the questions . . . the police came by twice last week.

BRAD: I'm sorry.

LYDIA: It's not your fault. Gives me an excuse to get out, move on. I'm thinking of going back to school. I want to work with people.

BRAD: You'd be good at that. You would. *(pause)* What time is it?

LYDIA: Three. Why? What's wrong?

BRAD: I have to take my pills. Where are they? Have you got them?

LYDIA: No. They must be in your room. Relax, Brad. We'll head back.

BRAD: I gave them to you, I'm sure I did. Aren't they in your purse? Check your purse. I HAVE TO TAKE MY PILLS!

LYDIA: It's o.k. We'll go back to your room, we'll find them. They have to be there.

BRAD: *(becoming hysterical)* I HAVE TO HAVE THEM! I HAVE TO HAVE MY PILLS! WHERE ARE THEY? WHERE ARE MY PILLS? I HAVE TO TAKE MY PILLS!

LYDIA *embraces* BRAD, *holds him.*

LYDIA: It's o.k., Brad, it's all right. We'll get them, you'll be all right.

BRAD: Please ... take me home, I wanna go home ... please ... Lydia ... please ...

LYDIA: We had everything, Brad. Everything we needed. But it was never enough. You were always looking for something? What was it, Brad? What were you looking for?

BRAD *moves slowly to centre stage and sits in front of the monitor.*

THE SHIV: Come on, Brad. Time's racin'. Tell her why, tell her what happened, tell us all what happened. Let's clear the air here.

BRAD: One little thing can turn it all upside down: a phone call, a letter, someone thinks they saw you there. Something happens, outside of yourself. Suddenly ... you're connected.

BETTY *moves downstage left and recites the following poem, accompanied by discordant piano chords.*

> *Love is a knife*

in the guts
Love
Like a knife
It hits
It hits
It hits

The lights come down slowly, spot remains on BRAD. *Piano joins in. The monitor shows the shot of the fire.* BETTY *moves off. The* STORYTELLER *approaches, gently sweeps his hand across* BRAD's *eyelids, shutting them. The* STORYTELLER *remains behind* BRAD, *looking down, hands folded in front of him. Spot begins to dim. Random slides resume, culminating with the funeral shots. Low sax in the background, lights dim to black.*

OTHER TITLES FROM ANVIL PRESS PUBLISHERS:

A Circle of Birds (A Novel)

by Hayden Trenholm

A Circle of Birds is an impressionistic, finely-wrought tale of lost memory, tangled history, despair and discovery. A journey through much Canadian and world history, an unrelenting yarn of death and twisted love, *A Circle of Birds* was chosen from some 250 entries as the winner of the 15th Annual International 3-Day Novel Contest. Available: Spring 1993.

ISBN: 1-895636-03-5

Stupid Crimes (A Novel)

by Dennis E. Bolen

Set in Vancouver, *Stupid Crimes* chronicles the urban universe of Barry Delta, a world-weary but compassionate parole officer.

> *" . . . a contemporary, experimental and imaginative treatment of very old themes."*
>
> —EVE DROBOT, *The Globe & Mail*

ISBN: 1-895636-01-9; $10.95 paper; 5½" x 8¼"; 178pp; 1992

A Toilet Paper or A Treatise on Four Fundamental Words Referring to Gaseous and Solid Wastes Together with Their Point of Origin

by Rachel Mines

A humorous examination, from a historical linguistic viewpoint, of four commonly-used words relating to our posterior orifice and that which comes out of it.

ISBN: 1-895636-00-0; $4.95 paper; 4½" x 5½"; 40pp; 1991

sub-TERRAIN Magazine

Always an eclectic mix of fiction, poetry, photography and art from uprising Canadian, American & International writers and artists. Alternately praised and denounced, *sub-TERRAIN* remains unmotivated by the patriotic urges of Nationalism, the prideful swoons of Regionalism or Canadian Unity. We are concerned with the forging of a personal identity in these present and troubled times. Home of The Penny Dreadful Short Story Contest & The Last Poems Poetry Contest.

ISSN: 0840-7533

NEW HOME OF THE ANNUAL INTERNATIONAL 3-DAY NOVEL-WRITING CONTEST (LABOUR DAY WEEKEND)